LASH BOX
VENDING
BUSINESS

LASH BOX VENDING BUSINESS

HOW TO START YOUR EYELASH VENDING BUSINESS

LEARN HOW TO MAKE THOUSANDS
MONTHLY SELLING EYELASHES &
ACCESSORIES IN A VENDING MACHINE.

WITH

TOP 10 WHOLESALE EYELASH VENDORS
& SUPPLIERS INCLUDED

Jeneita Green, MA

Disclaimer: In this book, you will learn my experience of how I made over a thousand dollars within the first month after placing my eyelash vending machine in its location. This is only my experience informing you about the steps I took to ensure the success of my machine. This book doesn't guarantee success; however, it gives the steps and tools you will need to do to reach your goals. For further assistance and consultation please contact me at info@beautyblessing.org.

Print information available on the last page.

Rev. date: 03/25/2021

To order additional copies of this book, contact:
Xlibris
844-714-8691
www.Xlibris.com
Orders@Xlibris.com
827914

CONTENTS

INTRODUCTION

Opening a vending machine business is a very interesting activity. *Let's face it ...*

Who would not like to start a profitable business that allows them to always obtain automatic earnings, with a few hours of work a day?

It is no coincidence that the vending machine business has seen constant growth in recent years ...

Vending machines are automatic shops that run for 24 hours per day, it can be used to sell eyelashes, makeup, hair extensions, condoms, PPEs, snacks, drinks, and more.

Today it is possible to sell practically anything, thanks to vending machines, with a rather interesting average profit.

So don't waste any more time ...

In this Ebook, I will explain the basic steps to start eyelashes vending machine business, the potential of the sector, how much eyelashes vending machine costs, the license necessary to start the business, marketing strategy, and the average earnings that you can expect to achieve with this type of business. You will also learn my experience of how I made over a thousand dollars within the first month after placing my eyelash vending machine in its location.

Are you ready?
Let's go!

UNDERSTANDING VENDING MACHINE BUSINESS

A vending machine business is a retail business that does not require face-to-face interaction with customers and can be run 24 hours a day, depending on the location. This business offers flexibility to operators as it can adapt to the owner's lifestyle, thereby creating a balance between work, life, and family. Entrepreneurs may also go into other businesses, while others may decide to make it a part-time business venture.

Vending machines are automatic vending machines for all kinds of grocery items and products such as snacks, hair, eyelashes, jewelry, mask makeup, and other beauty and skin products. The action of supplying these products through these machines is known internationally as "vending".

The vending machine business has become one of the world's fastest-growing and most profitable businesses. Several reasons explain the advantages and success of the vending machine business: from the consumer's point of view, the pace of life does not allow in many cases to take time to go for a coffee or go to buy the newspaper, eyelash or recharge the phone.

Having vending machines that supply these items at hand makes it easier for us to acquire them due to their easy display, wide assortment of products, supply points, prices, order, and classification, as well as saving us time.

More so, Life, especially in the city, is becoming increasingly hectic ...

Precisely for this reason, there are more and more those who have little time to devote to purchases and are looking for a quick and economical solution for their needs.

All the subjects belonging to these categories represent your future potential customers.

All you have to do is guarantee they always find, 24 hours a day, 7 days a week, a vending machine from which they can buy what they need on the fly!

In short, the products for vending machines that you can sell are many and the market is constantly growing.

As you can see, the earning possibilities are many and the sector is very promising!

And if you think about it, I'm sure you'll agree with me too ...

Nowadays the only certainty to take your life in hand and create a future is to start your own business.

Unfortunately, 9 out of 10 people fail in their project because they take it too lightly ... so to set up your business, you need to have a business idea, create a credible business plan and be ready to take responsibility.

TOP EXAMPLE OF VENDING MACHINE BUSINESS IDEAS

Starting a vending machine business is a sure way to take advantage of technology and retail to make money.

As I've explained earlier, vending machine business is a retail business that does not require face-to-face interaction with customers and can operate for 24 hours every day, depending on the location. This business offers flexibility to the operator because it can be adapted to suit the owner's lifestyle.

Leverage in the vending business consists of strategically placing the vending machines in a location that has the right amount of traffic, as well as ensuring that the vending machine has the right product for the traffic. If you are interested in starting a vending machine related business idea in your country, here are examples of vending business ideas that you can choose from comfortably;

1. Eyelashes vending machine business
2. Grocery vending machine business
3. Beverage vending machine business
4. Snack vending machine business
5. Children's toy vending machine business

6. Beauty and cosmetic product vending machine business
7. Event and lottery ticket vending machine business
8. Music and movie vending machine business
9. Cupcake vending machine business
10. Frozen food vending machine
11. Ice cream vending machine business
12. Hair extensions and hair care products vending machine business
13. Vending machine business of educational materials for children
14. Perfume vending machine business
15. Food supplement vending machine business
16. Stationery vending machine business
17. Newspaper and magazine vending machine business
18. Pizza vending machine business
19. Book vending machine business
20. Greeting card vending machine business

Advantage Of Vending Machine Business

The current trend in the business world is to undertake business as automatically as possible, to develop and do more activities at the same time. New technologies such as the Internet, or electronics make it possible.

That is why Vending has become fashionable again and in the sights of entrepreneurs. OK!

With vending machines, it is enough for one person to simply insert coins, bills, tokens, or cards and press a button or turn a knob to obtain the desired merchandise. The vending is born to satisfy the need for men to acquire all kinds of items in the best conditions of hygiene and quality, at any time and as soon as possible.

Vending has become one of the most lucrative and fastest-growing commercial activities in the world in recent times. An ingenious method of attracting resources, which can serve as a complementary source of your income, or it can also become your main economic activity.

The increasingly advanced electronic and mechanical systems that control automatic vending machines allow the successful and autonomous marketing of countless products.

Now let's see the main advantages:

1. **Vending machines sell all the time:** This is called 24/7, that is, they are shop windows open to the public 24 hours a day, 7 days a week. By itself, this is one of the main advantages of this business.

2. **It allows several businesses to be carried out at the same time:** Vending is compatible with other activities since by not needing the physical presence of a seller, he can carry out other undertakings.

3. **Requires little time:** This point is related to the previous one. It is a business that leaves a lot of free time for the entrepreneur. In case of having many dispensers, an employee or assistant can replace the products and take care of the maintenance, leaving the entrepreneur liberated.

4. **The entrepreneur has freedom of schedules and times:** It does not matter if you go on vacation or are sick, or one day it occurs to you to stay to sleep until later. Vending machines keep selling for you.

5. **They require less and less maintenance:** Until a few years ago, one of the main drawbacks of these machines was the high maintenance requirement. Thus a person who owned 100 machines needed to work too many hours per week in maintenance. Currently, an entrepreneur with this amount of equipment only requires about 15 hours a week in total.

6. **It is a business that is proof of crises and recessions:** As much as people's purchasing power decreases, they need to continue eating, drinking, a coffee, or a soda.

7. **You can start with very little investment:** Beyond the relatively low price of the machines, this business can be started with a single machine and increase the amount over time. So it is only necessary to reinvest the money in new machines. This way of working also makes it a low-risk business.

8. **An automatic vending machine is the ideal employee:** It does not require salaries, vacations, social services, it does not leave due to illness or request raises, it never complains, it does not have to pay compensation or wait for lawsuits. Just charge and deliver.

9. **The demand is constantly increasing:** In Japan, there is a surprising market for this sector, millions of machines in the main cities. In Latin America, it is just beginning to grow so it is the ideal time to invest in it.

10. **High profitability:** The absence of personnel and all the costs that it implies, the automation of the processes, and the lower maintenance required by current machines make the business increasingly profitable

It is for all these advantages that investment experts are recommending vending as one of the best investment options for the coming years.

WHO IS A VENDOR

A vendor, also known as a supplier, is an individual or company that sells goods or services to someone else in the economic production chain.

Vendors are a part of the supply chain: the network of all the individuals, organizations, resources, activities, and technology involved in the creation and sale of a product, from the delivery of source materials from the supplier to the manufacturer, through to its eventual delivery to the end-user.

Parts manufacturers are vendors of parts to other manufacturers that assemble the parts into something sold to wholesalers or retailers. Retailers are vendors of products to consumers. In information technology as well as in other industries, the term is commonly applied to suppliers of goods and services to other companies.

How a Vendor Works

A vendor, also known as a supplier, is a person or a business entity that sells something. Large retail store chains such as eyelash vending machine business, for example, generally have a list of vendors from which they purchase goods at wholesale prices that they then sell at retail prices to their customers.

Note:

- A vendor is a general term used to describe any supplier of goods or services.
- A vendor sells products or services to another company or individual.
- Large retailers rely on many different vendors to supply products, which it buys at wholesale prices and sells at higher retail prices.
- A manufacturer that turns raw materials into a finished good is a vendor to retailers or wholesalers.
- Some vendors, like food trucks, sell directly to customers.

Some vendors also can sell directly to the customer, as seen with street vendors and food trucks. Besides, a vendor can act as a business-to-business (B2B) sales organization that provides parts of a product to another business to make an end product.

Finally, a vendor supplies eyelashes of various types to you as an eyelash vending machine entrepreneur. Have the list of vendors around your location and you need to carefully select a vendor to do business with.

DIFFERENT TYPE OF EYELASHES

TYPES OF EYELASHES YOU SHOULD KNOW

In starting the eyelashes vending machine business, there is a need for you to know different types of eyelashes. Each type has its unique effects on your eyes and your overall appearance.

Mink Eyelashes

Mink eyelashes are the most common among celebrities. Minks are known for best achieving a natural-look because they are made from real hair. This type of eyelashes is suitable for those who are looking for a natural, light yet luscious look. Besides, mink eyelashes are very thin. As a result, they tend to last longer because they will not weigh down your natural eyelashes.

Faux Mink Eyelashes

Faux mink eyelashes are similar to mink eyelashes, just that they are synthetic. This type of eyelashes is ideal for those who want to achieve a natural look, similar to mink eyelashes, but at a lower cost. It is also suitable for those who do not want to use real hair. An advantage of this type of mink is that they will not lose their curl effect even when they get wet.

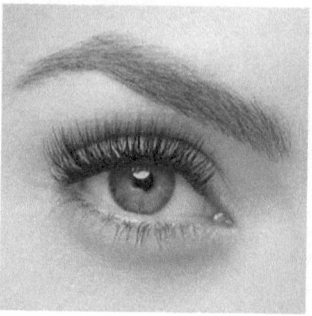 

Sable Eyelashes

Sable eyelashes are made from the fur of the Sable (a forest animal found in Russia and Siberia). Sable eyelashes are highly similar to mink eyelashes, except for the fact that sable eyelashes are the thinnest lashes of all types. This is ideal for those who appreciate naturally thin lashes and do not like thicker options. Sable eyelashes will not weigh down your natural eyelashes and can create a wispy look.

Silk Eyelashes

Silk eyelash is a combination between mink and synthetic, in terms of the natural look and thickness of the lashes. This type is special because they tend to be thicker at the bottom and gradually become thinner towards the end, giving you a fuller appearance of the lash line. Your eyelashes will look darker, fuller, and glossier. This type of eyelash is ideal for those who do not want to use real fur.

Synthetic Eyelashes

Synthetic lashes are for those who are looking for a bold, glamorous look. No real fur will be used for this type of eyelash extension. As a result, it will be significantly cheaper. After the synthetic eyelash extension, there won't be any need for mascara and other touch-ups, any longer!

Let's go through the top best 7 eyelash manufacturers in the U.S.A. Choose your supplier wisely!

Spa Lashes Expressive lash extensions with a 5.0 review rating on Yelp, Spa Lashes is a premium brand of eyelash extension services. Rated #1 in LA and voted thrice in a row by Burbank, Spa Lashes is recommended by celebrities Sabrina Carpenter and Madison Beer.

Dior Lashes

Wholesale mink lash vendor in the U.S.A, Dior Lashes feature all the accessories that a lash artist needs in their saloon. You will find 16 mm to 20mm and 25 mm mink lashes for wholesale purchase on Dior eyelash extensions.

Lash Box LA

An easy to navigate website boasting years of lash supplier experience, Lash Box eyelash manufacturer in Los Angeles offers lash training as well. The lash options on Lash Box are Mega volume, Russian Volume 8-10D, Volume 3-5D, Royal Sable Collection, Cashmere Lashes, Man Lashes, and Silky Mink.

Xtreme Lashes

Situated in Texas, Xtreme Lashes offers a wide range of lash accessories and extensions. You can choose from Classic eyelash extensions and Volume Eyelash Extensions on this eyelash manufacturer from the United States of America.

Be Lashes

One of the common places for buying eyelash extensions in Wholesale when in the U.S.A, Be Lashes is a specialist of 3D Mink

False Lashes. You can choose from different private label boxes too. Their hottest lashes are 3D Mink, 3D Velvet, and 50 types of eyelash extensions.

The Lash Labs

Situated in CA, Seattle, WA, and LA, Lash Labs is a popular lash supplier in the U.S.A. From bulk type lash to twinkle eyelashes, double tapered, glam eyelash, to mascara, The Lash Labs has the complete products for a lash salon in the U.S.A.

Misen Lashes

One of the best eyelash manufacturers U.S.A, Misen Lashes offers custom eyelashes with packaging options too. They have 20mm mink lashes, 25mm Siberian Mink lashes, 22mm mink lashes, and other lash salon accessories.

Top 10 wholesale eyelash vendors & suppliers

If you want to start your own fake eyelash brand business, then you must understand the top ten false eyelash supplier websites.

1. https://www.obeyabeauty.com/

    Qingdao Obeya beauty Products CO., Ltd

    Wholesale Mink Eyelashes Supplier, 100% Mink Eyelashes Manufacturer

    We offer the highest quality Mink eyelashes in the industry, all of our eyelashes are with 100% mink fur, and 100% handmade to exact specifications. And we have years of experience in OEM/ODM to supply you with custom eyelashes, private labels, and private packaging.

2. https://www.meideareyelash.com/

    Meidear eyelash

    Wholesale Mink eyelashes manufacturers, False eyelashes suppliers, China Eyelash extensions factory

    we are an eyelash factory and wholesaler, supply lashes worldwide, professional manufacturer and supplier of Mink eyelashes, False eyelashes, and Eyelash extensions.

3. https://www.emedaeyelash.com/

    Emeda Eyelash

    Eyelash Extension Supplies, wholesale mink eyelashes, China false eyelashes manufacturers

    We wholesale eyelashes worldwide. Emeda eyelash is a professional manufacturer and supplier of Eyelash Extension, mink eyelashes, false eyelashes, and fake eyelashes in China since 2002. We produce such as individual eyelashes,3D lashes, human hair eyelashes, etc.

4. https://www.obeyalashes.com/

    Obeya Lashes

    Silk eyelash extensions manufacturer, Mink eyelash extensions supplier

    Our Eyelash Extensions Factory is one of the leading wholesale eyelash extension manufacturers and the best silk/ mink eyelash extension wholesale suppliers in China.

5. https://www.elourlashes.com/

    Elour Lashes

    Wholesale 3D lashes manufacturers, mink eyelashes suppliers, China lash extensions factory

We are an eyelash factory, leading supplier and manufacture of mink eyelashes, eyelash extensions, false eyelashes products, etc, in China.

6. https://www.vendorseyelash.com/

Private Label Lashes and Packaging Factory

3D Mink Lashes Factory, wholesale Faux Mink lashes manufacturer,3D Silk lashes suppliers

We are private label mink lashes and packaging factory, Together with us, Start own lashes business.

7. https://sheeyelash.com/

She eyelash

Wholesale Eyelash extension manufacturers, Mink lashes suppliers, China Eyelashes factory. We are a wholesale Eyelash extension vendor, and we own a lashes factory. R&D and production of various styles of mink eyelashes, eyelash extensions false lashes in Qingdao, China.

8. https://www.imilashes.com/

Imi lashes

Wholesale Eyelash extensions vendors, mink lashes manufacturers, China false lashes suppliers

IMI Lashes is one of the most professional eyelash extensions, volume lash extensions; mink lashes manufacture and vendor in China.

9. https://www.hlashes.com/

They are a china fake eyelashes factory directly operated online mall, Wholesale eyelash vendors. Factory prices directly wholesale eyelash extensions, mink eyelashes, 3D lashes, human hair eyelashes, and so on false eyelashes. Brands with EMEDA Eyelashes, Obeya Eyelashes, and Meret top brand fake eyelashes. This is an EMEDA hair & lashes online store.

10. https://www.skyeyelash.com/

Qingdao Sky eyelash

Mink Eyelashes Wholesale|False Eyelashes|Eyelash Manufacturer

They offer Custom or Wholesale Mink Eyelashes Wholesale|False Eyelashes|Eyelash Manufacturer|Eyelash Extensions at …

Choose The Name Of Your Eyelash Vending Machine Business

Once you have concluded that your eyelash vending machine business idea may be feasible or has a chance of success, the next thing you could do is make one of the most important decisions you must make when starting a business: choosing the name of your business.

To choose the name of your business, the first thing you should do is identify two or more words that are related to it, and that you would like to include in the name; For example, if you are going to create a taxi company, and you would like to highlight the safety of your services, you could name it "Safe Taxi".

But in addition to words that are related to your business, other considerations that you should take into account when choosing the name of your business are:

Personal tastes: the name you choose for your business will be something that will accompany you for as long as it lasts, so you should choose a name that is to your liking and with which you feel a certain affinity.

Positive image: you should also choose an attractive name that generates a positive image, and that does not have a negative connotation or mean something bad in any language or culture.

Informative nature: it is recommended that the name not only be related to your business but also that it communicates or transmits something that you would like to highlight from it.

Easy pronunciation: it is also important that the name of your business is preferably short and easy to pronounce and remember.

That it is not registered: for you to be the only one who can use it, you must make sure that the name you have in mind is not already registered by other businesses.

Internet domain available: taking into account that today it is essential that your business has a website, you must also make sure that there is a domain available for the name you have in mind.

To get ideas for the name of your business, you could look at the names of your competition and pay attention to the ones you like the most, or go to business directories on the Internet that are of the same type as your business, and look for names that serve as inspiration.

If you find it difficult to find the ideal name for your eyelash vending machine business, keep in mind that there are specialized companies that you could hire to help you with this task.

Register Your Eyelashes Vending Machine Business Name To Protect It

Once you've settled on a name that you like, you need to protect it. There are four ways to register your business name. Each serves a different purpose; some may be legally required depending on the business structure and location.

1. The name of the entity protects it at the state level
2. Trademark protects you at the federal level
3. The name you operate under (DBA [Doing Business As]) does not give you any legal protection, but the law may require it
4. Domain name protects your company's website address

Each of these name registries has legal independence. Most small businesses try to use the same name for each type of registration, but they are not normally required to do so.

Four ways to register your business name

Entity name

The entity name can protect your business name at the state level. Depending on your business structure and location, the state may require you to register the name of the legal entity.

Your entity name is how the state identifies your business. Each state may have different rules on what the entity name and the use of company suffixes can be. Registration of a registered name is not allowed in most states; some states require that the entity name reflect the type of business it represents.

In most cases, registering your entity name protects your business and prevents someone else in the state from operating under the same entity name. However, there are exceptions to the status and business structure.

Check with your state for the rules for registering your business name.

Commercial brand

The trademark can protect the name of your company, goods, and services at the national level. Trademarks prevent other people in the same (or similar) industry in the United States from using registered names as trademarks.

For example, if you have an electronics company and you want to call it Springfield Electronic Accessories and call one of your products Screen Cover 5000, registering those names as trademarks would prevent other electronics or similar companies from using the same names.

In every state, businesses are subject to trademark infringement lawsuits, which can be very costly. That is why you should check possible company, product, and service names against the official trademark database maintained by the United States Patent and Trademark Office.

The name under which it operates (DBA)

You may need to register your DBA (also called business name, fictitious name, an assumed name) with the state, county, or city in which your business is located. Registering your DBA name does not in itself offer you any legal protection, but registration is required in most states if you use it. Some business structures require you to use one.

And even if you are not required to register a DBA, it is in your best interest to do so anyway. It allows you to do business under a different identity than your name or the legal name of your formal company. As a bonus, registering a DBA and obtaining a federal tax identification number (EIN) will allow you to open a business bank account.

In a state there may be several known companies with the same DBA, so your choice is less restricted. There is also more leeway in clarity of the company's role. For example, a small business owner could use Springfield Electronic Accessories as the entity name, but use Tech Buddy for their DBA. Just remember that trademark infringement laws also apply here.

Determine your DBA requirements for your specific location. These vary with the business structure and state, county, and municipality, so check with local government offices and websites.

Domain name

If you want your business to have an online presence, start by registering a domain name, also called a website address or URL.

Once you register your domain name, no one else can use it as long as you remain the owner. It's a great way to protect your brand's online presence.

If someone else has already registered the domain you wanted to use, don't worry. The domain name does not have to be the same as the legal name of the company, trademark, or DBA. For example, Springfield Electronic Accessories might register the domain name techbuddyspringfield.com.

You register your domain name through a registration service. Consult a directory of reputable registries to determine which are the safest, and then choose the one that offers the best combination of price and customer service. You will need to renew your domain registration periodically.

Apply For Licenses And Permits

List of legal documents you need to run eyelashes vending machine business

Depending on the laws and regulations in the state you will be operating from, the documents required for a vending machine business are very strict, but the basic documents that will be needed to operate a vending machine business are listed below:

- Business license
- Business tax regulations
- New vending machine license
- Sales and use tax permit
- Home occupation permit
- State withholding information packet
- Special permit for vending machines
- Self-employment tax
- Zoning license

OPEN A BUSINESS BANK ACCOUNT FOR YOUR EYELASH VENDING MACHINE BUSINESS

Open a business bank account when you are ready to start receiving and spending money on behalf of your business. It helps you comply with the laws and be protected. It also offers benefits to its customers and employees.

Benefits of business bank accounts

You should open a business bank account as soon as you begin receiving and spending money on behalf of your business. The most common business accounts are checking, savings, credit card, and merchant services. The merchant services account allows you to accept credit and debit card transactions from your customers.

You can open a business bank account as soon as you have your *employer identification number* (EIN).

Most business bank accounts offer benefits that standard personal bank accounts do not have.

Protection: Commercial banking offers limited personal liability protection, keeping your business funds separate from your funds. Merchant services also offer purchase protection to their customers and guarantee the security of their personal information.

Professionalism: Customers will be able to pay you with credit cards and write checks for your business, not directly for you. Also, you can authorize your employees to handle everyday banking tasks on behalf of the company.

Preparation: Business bank accounts generally have the option of a line of credit for the company. This can be used in an emergency or if the company needs new equipment.

Buying Power: Credit card accounts can help you make large purchases to start your business and help you establish your credit history.

Find an account with low commissions and high profits

Some entrepreneurs open a business account at the same bank that they use for their accounts. Rates, fees, and options vary by bank, so you should shop around to make sure you find the lowest fees and the best benefits.

Some factors to consider when opening a business checking or savings account are:

1. Opening offers
2. Interest rates on savings and checks
3. Interest rates on credit lines

4. Transaction fees
5. Commissions for early termination
6. Commissions for minimum account balance

Some factors to consider when opening a merchant account are:

1. Discount rate. The percentage they charge for each transaction processed.
2. Transaction fees. The amount they charge for each credit card transaction.
3. Commissions for the home verification service (AVS).
4. Daily batch processing fees in ACH. The commissions are charged when the day's credit card transactions are posted.
5. Minimum monthly commissions. The commission is charged if the company does not cover the required minimum number of transactions.

Payment processing companies are an increasingly accepted alternative to traditional merchant services accounts. Some offer additional features, such as accessories that allow you to use the phone to accept credit card payments. The commission categories you need to consider will be similar to those for merchant services accounts.

If you find a payment processor that you like, remember that you will still need to connect it to a business checking account to receive payments.

Have the documents you need to open a business bank account

It's easy to open a business bank account once you've selected the bank. Just go online or go to a bank branch to start the process.

These are some of the documents most commonly requested by the bank; some institutions can ask for more.

1. Employee *identification number* (**EIN**) (or social security number if you are the sole owner)
2. Articles of incorporation of your company
3. Property agreements
4. Business license

CHOOSE A BUSINESS STRUCTURE

The business structure you choose influences everything from day-to-day operations to paying taxes and risk to your assets. You must choose a business structure that gives you the right balance of legal protections and benefits.

The structure of your business influences the amount of taxes you will pay, your ability to obtain money, the documentation you need to submit, and your responsibilities.

You need to choose a commercial structure to register your company with the State. Most businesses also need to obtain a tax identification number and apply for the necessary licenses and permits.

Choose carefully. Although the commercial structure could change later, there may be restrictions by location. This could also have tax consequences and lead to involuntary dissolution, among other complications.

It may be helpful to consult with business advisers, lawyers, and accountants.

Various categories of business structure are Sole proprietorship Partnerships, Limited Liability Partnerships, Limited Liability Company (LLC) Corporations

Corporation C S corporation B corporation Close corporation Nonprofit corporations, cooperative.

Getting The Right And Best Location For Eyelash Vending Machine

As previously mentioned, the key factor in the success of this type of business is its location.

Therefore you will agree with me that making a careful analysis of the place where to place your automatic shop is essential!

So let's see this fundamental aspect together:

Where to open your vending machine?

Those who make this kind of purchase are almost always people who have little time available.

Often these are men and women who work and in addition to work have an active life either because they have small children or because they carry out activities related to well-being and leisure.

Not to be underestimated is the range of young students who dedicate themselves to fun and social relations in the evening.

In general, therefore, places, where a greater number of people and activities are concentrated, are to be preferred.

On the other hand, small towns or, in cities, the so-called dormitory districts where you return only to go home after work are not recommended.

Also, your typical customer may be looking for a particular product that is not sold by anyone in your area and can only be found in your vending machine. Or you want a cheaper solution than that of the nearest shop. Or even shop at night when traditional shops are closed, and your 24-hour distributor is there to meet their needs.

As you can see, it's always about understanding what your potential customer is looking for, and meeting their needs!

Where and how to place the business.

In order not to receive an immediate refusal, it is good to try to understand which location is available to start the franchise. A small restaurant in a mountain village does not have the same appeal (for customers and) as a large space in a central area of any city. So it appears logical as:

- square footage
- position
- urban context
- presence or absence of competition

can be extremely decisive factors in understanding which product sector you can think of distributing. As we will see in a few lines, for example, there are franchises of distributors of games and sweets that are "accompanied" by a play area for the little ones. In such a context, for example, a lot of space is needed.

Then, the geographical position turns out to be a factor of incredible importance. Opening the business on a road with a lot of pedestrian traffic can be very important, but having a parking lot a few meters away can also be useful. Shopping centers, malls, schools, railway stations, banks, offices of the Public Administration or in any case areas near very busy shops are generally excellent locations (always as long as there is no competition).

How do I get the spaces?

You should know that the owner of an area seeks to make their spaces profitable, but is not willing to lease it to anyone willing to pay for it. You must inspire trust; convey honesty and responsibility, and a clear vision of your business.

If you have already looked for spaces and you know your suppliers, the next thing is to ask for a meeting with the manager, administrator, or owner of the place.

Many people find this part very difficult they cannot believe that a few years ago and without experience, I would have managed to talk to who is the boss in a shopping center.

For this, I have a super powerful secret that a friend taught me who always managed to access very important and difficult people to approach. If you want to talk to the most important person in the place, ask who he is and ask to speak to him.

Yes, you got it right, that's the super-secret, if you want something ask for it, it's that simple. Now, if you want it to be more complicated, I could think of something, but I recommend keeping it simple.

There are three basic steps to open the doors and start your negotiation:

1. Ask who's the boss
2. Offers to monetize spaces and improve customer service
3. Set up a post-meeting

Do you remember what any owner or space manager looks for? Whether you are a small business owner or manager of a large shopping center, you cannot afford to make your spaces profitable at any cost. The manager must ensure the service and experience of customers. That is, if the manager of a shopping center sees the opportunity to generate income by renting a space for the sale of junk food in a place for athletes at a very good price, he is probably destined to fail since he will sacrifice the visits of his target audience to win. a great short-term income.

That said, what do you think you can offer a space owner to install your future vending machines? Exactly! Improve customer service.

The next step then is to go for your space!

Your offer will be that the owner will make a profit from your leases and that you will provide a very attractive service to customers, who frequent the place, whether with soda machines, sweets, photographs, rides, or whatever your dispensing machine business is about.

Remember well, make your spaces profitable and improve the service to your customers. That phrase is music to the ears of an owner or manager of the space you want.

This is what I would recommend that you say to him: "Hello, are you Mr. Maxwell? (for example). My name is (your name) and I am a frequent customer of this shopping center (note that by presenting yourself as a customer you gain hierarchy in front of your interlocutor). I am dedicated to the vending machine business and I would like to offer you the opportunity to make your spaces profitable and to improve the experience of your customers."

This presentation can lead you to the following options:

He was very interested and wants to speak immediately on the subject. In this case, you ask him if he can give you a half-hour of his full attention so that you can tell him about your project.

- He asks you for more information but shows no interest. Although it is not the same as the previous case, the output is the same, that is, request a meeting where he can give you a few minutes of his maximum attention.
- He tells you that he is not interested. At this point tell him that you appreciate his frankness and that he receives your card in case he may require your services in the future.

Note that in any of the different situations, you never have a hall meeting or a quick meeting.

For this meeting your preparation is essential. You need to take printed photos of the machines offered by your supplier and be prepared with what you want and are willing to give up. For example, you have to be prepared for the following questions: how much rent do you want to pay? When can we start? Do your machines use a lot of electricity? Where else do you have more machines installed? How long have you been in business?

Prepare for the worst and hope for the best and always remember to maintain your entrepreneurial position and that you are not asking for a favor, you are looking for allies for your interesting project, showing yourself friendly, confident, and willing to collaborate.

Write A Business Plan For Your Eyelash Vending Machine Business

Any serious-minded entrepreneur knows that you need a detailed business plan, no matter how easy the business may seem. Business analysts have continually emphasized the need for a well-thought-out plan for how the business will run. The business plan can vary widely depending on how complex the business will be. no entrepreneur should invest their time and money in a business they intend to start or buy without seeing clear guidance on how the business will be run and how it will generate profits.

Eyelash vending machine business is no different even though the business does not require the constant presence of the owner and may not require an elaborate business plan; You need a business plan anyway. A business plan is a detailed and clear guide that a serious entrepreneur needs to run a business, and shows the strategies and objectives that the business intends to achieve over the life of the business.

A business plan requires certain information that must be contained in the document, and entrepreneurs who have found writing a business plan daunting have hired business plan writers to help them establish clear guidance, or browse the internet and download a template, the sample that would make writing a business plan easier, especially if you are trying to minimize upfront cost.

A business plan should have the following key components; The goal of starting the vending machine business, how you intend to generate seed capital or what capital is on hand, attract more traffic, where you intend to locate the vending machine to maximize its use, and how many vending machines you plan to own and operate.

Other information that should be included includes; a description of what your eyelash vending machine business is about, your company's vision, mission, short-term and long-term business goals; your marketing and sales strategies, especially in regards to how you intend to attract traffic, how you intend to boost your brand and create awareness for your vending machine, what strategies exist to effectively compete with other vending machines in the same location or with the same products, what products or niche ideas for your vending machine you will offer, SWOT analysis, your financial projections for at least 3 and maximum 5 years, your advertising and customer retention strategy, etc.

Financing Your Eyelash Vending Machine Business

Financing a business from scratch is not easy for any entrepreneur, and the hassles in this process have led to a shortage of many business ideas and startups. Most of the time, your savings may not cover a quarter of the financial requirements for a new business, and that's when your business plan can be used to raise funds from elsewhere. This is why you always make sure that your business plan be clear and provide concise strategies on how you intend to operate and grow your business.

It costs money to start a business. Financing your eyelash vending machine business is one of the first (and most important) decisions business owners make. How you decide to finance your business can affect how it is structured and operated.

Determine how much financing you will need.

Every business has different needs and there is no one financial solution that fits all. Your financial situation and vision for your eyelash vending machine business will determine the financial future of your business.

Once you know how much startup financing you will need, it is time to assess how you will get there.

There are several options available to those who want to finance the start of their eyelash vending machine business, and they include:

- Small business administration loan (SBA)
- Bank financing
- Home equity loan
- Family loan
- Using money from your tax return
- Obtaining business startup financing from vending machine vendors
- Selling unused and unnecessary items
- Bottling companies alternative financing options
- Lease purchase
- Personal savings (Finance your business with your funds)Also called *bootstrapping*, self-financing allows you to leverage your financial resources to support your business.

Self-financing can consist of turning to family and friends for capital, using your own savings accounts.

With self-financing, you retain full control of the business, but you also bear all the risk yourself. Make sure you don't spend more than you can afford, especially if you decide to use your retirement accounts prematurely. You may face costly fees or fines, or damage your ability to retire on time, so check with your plan administrator and personal financial advisor first.

What Does It Take To Start A Vending Machine Business?

Before starting the eyelash vending machine business, there are certain questions you will need to answer to get an idea of what you are trying to accomplish. The questions are:

1. Do you intend to go into business as a part-time or full-time owner?

2. Will, you be a sole operator, will you partner with someone, or will you buy a franchise?

3. How much capital is needed and how much is available and where would you need to get the finances for the business?

4. What are your short, medium, and long-term goals?

5. What kind of machines would you need to get? Would they be new or used?

6. Are you buying an existing route or starting over by securing your routes?

7. What are the existing policies and laws regarding the eyelash product?

8. What is my financial budget?

9. Who am my targeting? Gender, age etc?

10. Where will I locate my eyelash vending machine?

11. What are my plans to satisfying my customer?

As an entrepreneur, you need to be aware of existing policies and laws regarding the product you intend to enter. This is especially pertinent to your location. Any entrepreneur that wanted to start an eyelash vending machine business must give a detailed answer to the above question. These well prepared our mind to take responsibility for what matters and in every phase of your business, you will know the exact step to take. Remember, adequate preparation prevents poor performance.

Before I started this business, I spent time educating myself on different eyelash styles, sizes, cases, and vending machines. I spoke with several companies that customized vending machines to my needs. I narrowed it down to one of three companies that I wanted to do business with.

The machine developers and I spent time discussing the sizes and looks of the machine I wanted. I hired a graphic designer to explore the appearance I wanted for the machine.

Also during that time, I purchased sample mink eyelashes from several makers in search of those that were high quality, reusable, luxurious, cruelty-free, and have a natural look and feel. This process took patience because I wanted to make sure I was able to establish rapport and communication with vendors and choose lashes that would fit my customer lashes. I choose several types of lashes for my machine(over 30+styles). The idea is to keep my customers interest. Just like visiting a candy store, I wanted to be able to give customers several different choices to choose from.

I don't want my customers to get bored with the lashes in the machine so I plan to add different styles monthly.

The production and delivery of the machine took two months. Within that time frame, I spent time finalizing my contract with space at a mall and purchasing insurance for the machine per mall requirements. Space included a yearly rental and payment of $350 monthly (please note rental rates will vary based on location.)

Keep in mind, you must have an Employee Identification Number(EIN) assigned by the IRS, DBA, business license, and or reseller permit assigned by your state. This may also vary based on your state and location as having explained earlier. I was able to secure a location by contacting the specialty leasing agent at the mall. Every mall has a leasing agent. To find this information, go to the mall's website, stroll down to the bottom of the home page, and look for a specialty leasing agent or leasing agent. You can contact them through phone calls or email. Always send emails from your business account. You won't make sure you display professionalism at all times.

The type of vending machine you create is only limited by your imagination. All you need to do is figure out what you want to vend, how you want to brand your machine, what style of machine you desire, and the size of the items you wish to place in the machine. Examples of items to vend besides snacks and sodas are lipgloss/lipsticks, jewelry, PPEs, mink eyelashes, hair extensions, hair accessories, and other beauty products. Finding the right machine developers or vendors is the key to successful vending. On my website, I offer additional services such as providing one on one 1 hour consultation and mink eyelash and eyelash machine vendors available for purchase.

Please go to my website at www.beautyblessing.org for this opportunity and information.

How much does it cost to start a vending machine business?

The cost of starting a vending machine business is not fixed, it varies based on several factors such as how many vending machines the entrepreneur is willing to start, whether he wants to get new or refurbished machines, the location of the machines, and how far he is from the owner and many other factors.

This is the reason why an entrepreneur should always try to get the minimum initial cost so that he can recoup the initial investment faster.

The detailed breakdown of the expected costs is just a guide, as the cost of the vending machine varies depending on the product you want to offer to your customers.

Machine cost and overhead

The fact that business people require custom vending machines to suit the type of vending business they want to start makes vending machine manufacturing a good business to pursue. If you have the startup capital or technical training related to vending machine manufacturing, then by all means you should consider going into eyelash vending machine production.

The cost of the machine will vary from $2800 and up. My machine was created by a company located outside the US. Based on what your machine developer offer, you will also pay custom fees which will vary from $1000 -$1500 depending on the state where the machine will be delivered. All machines made outside of the US will be delivered through sea freight to major city shipping ports.

You may also have the machine delivered directly to your home, company location, or you can pick it up yourself from the port warehouse. Please note, if your machine vendor doesn't provide delivery as a free service, you will be responsible for covering this cost. We delivered our machine to the mall by purchasing a lift gate truck to transport and a four-wheel hand truck to move it from the truck to our mall space. Total tools and delivery cost was $1350. Please be sure to get a clear understanding of all costs from your vendor before making a machine purchase. Good communication with your vendor is extremely important throughout the entire process.

Eyelash Vending Machine Cost
Additional information

Currently, the insurance I have for my machine is from Hartford Insurance which is $49 per month. The insurance coverage is 1,000,000,000. Your insurance coverage requirements will vary by location. You can always check other companies like State Farm, Progressive, or other local insurance agencies that meet both your location and your needs. However, the cost of an eyelashes vending machine varies.

How to contact machine developers/vendors

After researching and receiving information about reputable specialty vending machine makers, I made contact through email and Whatsapp which is a free app you can download to your phone to connect with anyone across the world without paying any fees. There are vendors both domestic and international. I chose international due to the customize option available to purchase I was able to look at different machines and choose one to my desire. My machine is not the average design, style, and size vending machine. Please keep in mind before making any purchases you want to make sure you have a clear understanding of what you want.

Good communication leads to a successful transaction. Also, keep in mind international time zones which will be different from domestic time zones which will cause delays in responses. Ask the seller their location and Google the time zone. I made sure I wrote down at least 5 questions a day and sent them to the seller because I knew it could be to 6 hours before I received a response. My seller was prompt and sometimes responded within minutes no matter what time it was which made me feel confident in my purchase.

As with any business, anytime you feel a company is extremely late with responding, rude, and/or not providing you with enough information, please seek another vendor. Always ask your vendor to see samples of their work. After reviewing their work, I looked for other customers' information such as emails and social media sites on the machine shown and contact them to hear their experiences. This was one of the best ways for me to know that I was not being scammed.

Always ask about the store policy and production/shipping/ and delivery time so you can keep track of the process. Due to the pandemic, there was a delay in delivery by one week. I was informed less sea freight ships are moving at this time therefore I expected some delay.

Asking questions is a must not only to your vendor but other men or women who own an eyelash vending machine. Be prepared to pay someone for their time. You must develop a mind to invest in your business no matter what.

Maintenance of the eyelash vending machine

Always keep your machine clean. We use Windex for the glass and disinfected sprays and wipes to clean all areas of the machine, especially where customers are placing their hands and fingers. We also added a hand sanitizer station right beside the machine for safety and protection during this pandemic. This station can be purchased on Amazon.com. My machine contains 720pcs which is the maximum amount that can be added. Mink eyelashes length in our machine is 18mm to 30mm we also included mink eyelashes kit sets (mink eyelashes, diamond eyelash glue pens, tweezers, and brushes). The sets will give customers full access to everything they will need to put on their eyelashes.

The fastest selling products in our machine are the 20mm, 25mm, and mink eyelash sets. Additionally, as part of great customer service, we added a card reader by Nayax. This device was purchase when we bought our machine. The machine developers placed the card reader on the machine and added an account. This feature allows customers to pay with a debit/credit card or mobile phone. Through the Nayax app, we can check transactions on each product daily. This feature must be registered to your name and bank account. Once you get signed in and linked with an account, you are all set to add all your products to the device. I can explain more of this in detail during one on one 1-hour session which is available to purchase on our website www.beautyblessing.org.

How much I've made since placing my eyelash vending machine?

Let's just say I haven't had my machine for an entire month yet and I've made $1K without any marketing. I am hopeful by the time the machine gets the attention it needs and marketing takes off, it will make up to $6k monthly in revenue based on the inventory placed in the machine. I expect the money I paid to get this machine placed will be paid off within only a couple of months.

Frequent Asked Question

Does the eyelash vending machine business need intellectual property protection?

A vending machine distributes products, of whatever type, that are stored inside someone who needs them after pressing a button for that item; intellectual property is not required for this act.

However, if you come up with a new idea for your eyelash vending machine, either by changing its shape or creating a better way for the products to be distributed, then the business would need intellectual property protection and, in this case, a patent. A patent protects a new and not obvious novelty.

A business eyelash vending machine needs professional certification?

No, anyone who wants to get into the eyelash vending business does not require professional certification. This is one of the companies where, as an entrepreneur, you don't need to be near your machine all day, giving you time to venture into other tasks. You can also hire someone to make sure that the products are in the machine, and that there is no problem regarding the breakdown of the machine. Your employee also does not require certification.

DEFINE YOUR
TARGET MARKET

One of the most important steps in starting a business that many entrepreneurs often overlook is defining your target market; that is, the set of consumers to whom they will be directed.

Clearly defining your target market will allow you to adapt your product and orient your marketing efforts to the consumer that makes it up, and thus achieve greater efficiency than you would if you were targeting all the consumers that exist for your type of product.

For example, by defining your target market, you will be able to design a product that adapts to the tastes and preferences of the consumer that forms it and, therefore, a more effective product than one aimed at all consumers that do not take into account tastes and preferences.

To define your target market, it is recommended that you first segment the total market that exists for your type of product in different homogeneous markets made up of consumers with similar characteristics, and then choose the most attractive among the resulting markets to enter.

Some examples of target markets are:

1. Women 18 to 35 years of age with an average income of US $ 500 to the US $ 1,500.
2. Internet users looking to learn how to start their businesses.
3. Young students who tend to frequent discos and bars.
4. Older adults who do not have family members with enough time to care for and care for them.

One piece of advice at this point is that you define a target market that is not so broad since it would practically be as if you had not defined it; but not that specific either, since it would not be a market with enough buyers and, therefore, a sufficiently profitable market.

THE MARKETING PLAN

Marketing is extremely important in the eyelash vending machine business. Many were amazed when they saw the machine which helped tremendously with marketing. Most of the attention the machine gets is at the mall; however, I also use billboards, social media, word of mouth, and mall marketing. Create a Facebook, Instagram, and Pinterest business page for your machine and purchase ads. Also, every mall has a marketing department. Make sure you contact them for information on what services they can provide to assist in advertising your business. You will need to add this as part of your overhead cost for your business. Also, consider getting professional photos and videos of your machine. This will be needed for advertisement.

The correct marketing channels for a business are necessary and can sometimes be modified to suit a particular business, such as the eyelash vending machine business. That is why a business plan helps articulate the marketing strategies and ideas that would be used for a business.

Marketing your business accomplishes two things; generates income for your eyelash vending machine business and also increases publicity for your company or business.

An entrepreneur needs to take this aspect seriously, either by researching deeply and extensively, seeking the help of experienced owners in the same industry, and/or seeking the help of a consultant to help make marketing ideas viable for the business. intended target market.

Here are some marketing ideas and strategies for your eyelash vending machine business:

a. Print brochures about your vending machine and its location, or give your vending machine a unique look by painting it in bright colors or putting up a large neon sign so customers can easily recognize it.

b. Internet advertising on blogs and forums, and also on social media such as Twitter, Facebook, LinkedIn to get your message across, so that those on social media or reading blogs can know where to go, if they need a quick snack, especially if their Vending machine business deals with snacks.

c. Creating a basic website for your business, to give your business an online presence.

d. Advertising in local newspapers and magazines, or appropriate magazines that are related to the stock offered by the vending machine. For example, a vending machine that offers fresh and healthy food may advertise in local food or farmers' magazines.

e. Market directly the services offered by your vending machine.

f. Join local vending machine associations for industry trends and tips.

g. Attend seminars that would help improve your vending machine business. These seminars could be for business marketing best practices or other similar seminars.

h.   Give your customers discount days, even for products that don't sell well.

Factors to Help You Get the Right Product Price for Your eyelash Vending Machine Business

The main factor that will ensure that you provide the correct product price for your products and services in your vending machine is to keep your operating expenses as low as possible. the products in a vending machine are the same price, especially if your vending machine of popular product brands, but if your machine is selling unique products like niche shakes or services like tattoos, get the right price that will be affordable for customers, while keeping it afloat is to use the least amount of business operations without compromising certain qualities, such as getting a vending machine from a good brand.

Possible competitive strategies to beat your competitors in an eyelash vending machine industry

The fact that there are competitors in an industry proves that there is a market to be exploited and a demand to be met. Having competitors is therefore not necessarily a bad sign.

However, to be able to stand out from rival eyelash vending machine business, it is essential to know how to identify and know them. It is only by carrying out this competitive study that you will be able to gain a relevant competitive advantage.

Conducting a differentiation strategy is the key to winning over new customers, gaining market share, increasing turnover, and ensuring satisfactory profitability. When setting up a business, this step is all the more important since it makes it possible to achieve its competitive benchmark and thus to find its differentiating positioning and determine its key success factors.

Competition is good for business and helps a business stay proactive in looking for ways to get ahead of the competition. The products offered by eyelash vending machines are generally low priced due to the low cost of operation used in running the business, such as not paying for retail space, so there is no competitive pricing strategy that can be used against the competition, except for niche products or services.

The first competitive strategy may be to give your eyelash vending machine unique colors that make it immediately identifiable, so that it does not mix with other vending machines in the same location, but rather stands out. Also, your eyelash vending machine must be able to solve a problem for customers, such as saving time.

Another competitive strategy is to add services that your competitors or even regular retail stores are not offering. Additional services will not only increase sales but also customer loyalty to the brand.

Identifying your competitors, diagnosing their strengths and weaknesses to identify a differentiating positioning is essential to gain market share and increase turnover. Once they are identified, it is necessary to monitor them to always remain competitive.

Possible Ways to Increase Customer Retention for an Eyelash Vending Machine Business

The vending machine business is different from other types of businesses when it comes to retaining customers, especially since it is a machine that represents you or your brand. To build lasting relationships and retain your customers, you would need to provide excellent customer service.

One of the best ways to retain customers is to make sure your eyelash vending machines don't break down by performing preventative maintenance, or even if they do, they get repaired quickly.

This act will save your reputation and show your seriousness in retaining your customer;

a. You can have customers submit preferred share requests and then vote, with the highest votes for a share included in the vending machine. This is a good way to interact with customers, as well as to build a customer base for the vending machine.

b. Another way to retain your customers is to ensure that you provide only the best products in your eyelash vending machine, to ensure that your customers get the best.

c. Make sure your customers receive new product alerts on your machine by using a colorful sticker, giving incentives periodically or on special occasions, or hanging around after restocking to pass the information on.

Strategies to increase your brand awareness and create a corporate identity for your eyelash vending machine business.

The goal of developing strategies that drive your brand is so that the strengths of the products and the company can be emphasized. This means positioning yourself aggressively but innovatively in places like trade shows, on the Internet, and within the industry.

As an entrepreneur, you would have to realize that it is more costly to attract a new client than to retain one, and any entrepreneur who cannot handle this part of the business may need to hire a consultant to help as this is an aspect of business that cannot be overlooked.

Here are the strategies you would need to increase your brand awareness and create a corporate identity for your eyelash vending machine business:

a. First of all, your company's mission statement should drive your brand as it provides guidance for the employee who through their actions helps increase awareness of your brand.

b. Your marketing goals should be clear and strategic, such as a quarterly increase in market penetration, and also increase brand awareness by getting customer feedback and feedback.

c. Financial goals should be defined with customers in mind, which could be a lower but more effective cost of acquiring customers. This could take the form of giving discounts on certain products.

d. Another strategy is to position yourself by taking advantage of your strengths to have a competitive advantage over other competitors.

e. Lastly, brands can be driven by a continued increase in market penetration, developing a customer base, and building strong customer loyalty.

Find an eyelash supplier/distribution network for your eyelash vending machine business.

Regardless of whether you own just one or more eyelash vending machines, you would need a network of vendors or distributors that does your job of sourcing products or getting the products available on time for your customers.

This means having a good business relationship with these distributors, as it will help you to be more trustworthy with your customers, especially when it comes to filling the machine immediately when the products are finished. If the right relationship is cultivated, distributors could not only assist in the timely delivery of products but also convey certain information that could be beneficial to your business and help retain customers.

Daily Operation When Starting An Eyelash Vending Machine Business.

The daily operation is very simple. I summarize it in these points

1. Check that the machine has sufficient stock of product. And if not, replace those that have a low level of stock. This prevents the product from running out, thereby losing sales.
2. Withdraw the collection of the machine, coins, and/or bills.
3. Check the coin box and replace coins in the change tubes if necessary.
4. Check that the charging devices are working correctly.
5. Exterior cleaning of the machine (a clean and well-lit machine, sells more and offers more confidence)
6. Purchase of supplies. Take advantage of the offers of the different providers.

Tips For Successfully Running An Eyelash Vending Machine Business

Operating an eyelash vending machine may seem like an easy business, but it can be quicksand for entrepreneurs who mismanage the business. To run this business successfully, it would be necessary to create a template that would not only help the owner but also those who could be employed as well.

The first thing to always remember is that the customer is king, and give them the best treatment by not being lazy to fill the machine on time. The easiest way for your business to fail is not to worry about whether your machine is empty or full.

Also, make sure the machine is kept clean and in good repair. If you have a problem, it should not be out of service for a long period.

Another tip for successfully running a vending machine is to make sure the machines are kept in the best and most accessible locations, a location that does not disturb the customer when they intend to use the machine.

In conclusion, even if you already have a job or business of any kind,opening a vending machine can be an excellent addition to your traditional earnings and allow you to indulge in a few more whims at the end of the month!

Don't waste any more time, study these strategies and start working on creating your new business right away.

Best of luck and lots of automatic earnings!
A hug.

ABOUT THE AUTHOR

I'm Jeneita Green, MA. I have a bachelor's degree in Sociology and a master's degree in mental health counseling. After 17 years of working in a career of mental health and drug addiction, I fired my boss to start my hair care and beauty business. After selling wigs for so many years, I received many questions from my customers about purchasing mink eyelashes. I decided to incorporate mink eyelashes into my business. After several days of researching, I learned the business was saturated, I wanted to do something different. My husband and I started a snack, soda, and candy machine vending business for our son and we joined various vending machine groups on social media. I developed a love for mink eyelashes and working in the vending machine business. So we decided to link the two together and developed an eyelash vending machine.

ARE YOU INTERESTED IN STARTING AN EYELASH VENDING MACHINE BUSINESS?

HERE'S THE ASSISTANCE BEAUTY BLESSING CAN PROVIDE

- One on one phone consultation for $75
- Purchase a mink eyelash vendor $50
- Eyelash Vending Machine Vendor for $150

INFO@BEAUTYBLESSING.ORG   WWW.BEAUTYBLESSING.ORG

 BEAUTYBLESSINGWIGSNC    BEAUTYBLESSINGS6

www.ingramcontent.com/pod-product-compliance
Lightning Source LLC
Chambersburg PA
CBHW030940240526
45463CB00015B/838